Air Fryer Oven Cookbook

Easy and mouthwatering recipes. Get lean and lose weight with no-fuss recipes from beginners to advanced

TASHA MANN

© Copyright 2021 - All rights reserved.

TABLE OF CONTENTS

Introduction

With technology giving birth to different and unique inventions every day to satisfy the hunger for innovation in society, the everyday kitchen's modernization is also seen. Among the many devices that have made life more comfortable with their usefulness and design, the Air Fryer is an excellent tool with many benefits.

An Air Fryer is a device that cooks food not by using oil but by heated air with no compromise on the dish's texture and flavor. Air Fryer is not only used for frying up food, but can also be used for many other tasks such as grilling, baking, roasting, and many more. It ensures the food is cooked evenly and thoroughly. Its design is such that it fits in a compact area and works via electricity. It has many different parts:

The frying basket: It is a stainless-steel basket in which the food is placed for cooking. It can be replaced by any other utensils, such as a pizza pan.

The timer: The timer is set accordingly; a red light indicates when the time has been finished.

The temperature controller: The temperature of the Air Fryer has a high range from 175 to 400F. Adjust the temp knob to achieve the desired temperature.

The air inlet/outlet: It is used to release the hot air and steam that arises during the cooking process from the device's back. It is, therefore, important that the device is always kept in a spacious area.

How to Start Cooking in An Air Fryer?

Firstly, the Air Fryer must be in a spacious place to allow heat to escape and prevent damage to its parts. It should be put on top of a heat resistance surface.

Secondly, pull out the frying basket gently from the machine. It is recommended to preheat the device for 5 minutes before using it. Simply set the desired temperature for 5 mins and then after the time is completed, pull out the basket.

Now place the food inside the container. Not more than 2/3 of the container should be filled. If required, the container can be greased with an oil spray to avoid sticking the food. If fatty foods are placed, add a little bit of water so that the container remains clean.

CHAPTER 1

Breakfast

1.   Flax Meal Porridge

Preparation Time: 10 minutes

Cooking Time: 8 minutes

Servings: 4

Ingredients:

2 tbsp. sesame seeds

½ tsp.vanilla extract

1 tbsp. butter

1 tbsp. liquid Stevia

3 tbsp. flax meal

1 cup almond milk

4 tbsp. chia seeds

Directions:

Preheat your air fryer to 375°Fahrenheit. Put the sesame seeds, chia seeds, almond milk, flax meal, liquid Stevia and butter into the air fryer basket tray.

Add the vanilla extract and cook porridge for 8-minutes. When porridge is cooked stir it carefully then allow it to rest for 5-minutes before serving.

Nutrition:

Calories 298

Fat 26.7g

Carbs 13.3g

Protein 6.2g

2.   Scrambled Pancake Hash

Preparation Time: 7 minutes

Cooking Time: 9 minutes

Servings: 7

Ingredients:

1 egg

¼ cup heavy cream

5 tbsp. butter

1 cup coconut flour

1 tsp. ground ginger

1 tsp. salt

1 tbsp. apple cider vinegar

1 tsp. baking soda

Directions:

Combine the salt, baking soda, ground ginger and flour in a mixing bowl. In a separate bowl, crack the egg into it. Add butter and heavy cream. Mix well using a hand mixer.

Combine the liquid and dry mixtures and stir until smooth.

Preheat your air fryer to 400°Fahrenheit. Pour the pancake mixture into the air fryer basket tray.

Cook the pancake hash for 4-minutes. After this, scramble the pancake hash well and continue to cook for another 5-minute more. When the dish is cooked, transfer it to serving plates, and serve hot!

Nutrition:

Calories 178

Fat 13.3g

Carbs 10.7g

Protein 4.4g

3.   Morning Time Sausages

Preparation Time: 10 minutes

Cooking Time: 12 minutes

Servings: 6

Ingredients:

7 oz. ground chicken

7 oz. ground pork

1 tsp. ground coriander

1 tsp. basil, dried

½ tsp. nutmeg

1 tsp. olive oil

1 tsp. minced garlic

1 tbsp. coconut flour

1 egg

1 tsp. soy sauce

1 tsp.sea salt

½ tsp. ground black pepper

Directions:

Combine the ground pork, chicken, soy sauce, ground black pepper, garlic, basil, coriander, nutmeg, sea salt, and egg. Add the coconut flour and mix the mixture well to combine. Preheat your air fryer to 360°Fahrenheit.

Make medium-sized sausages with the ground meat mixture. Spray the inside of the air fryer basket tray with the olive oil. Place prepared sausages into the air fryer basket and place inside of the air fryer. Cook the sausages for 6-minutes.

Turn the sausages over and cook for 6-minutes more. When the cook time is completed, let the sausages chill for a little bit. Serve warm.

Nutrition:

Calories 156

Fat 7.5g

Carbs 1.3g

Protein 20.2g

4. Baked Bacon Egg Cups

Preparation Time: 10 minutes

Cooking Time: 12 minutes

Servings: 2

Ingredients:

2 eggs

1 tablespoon chives, fresh, chopped

½ teaspoon paprika

½ teaspoon cayenne pepper

3-ounces cheddar cheese, shredded

½ teaspoon butter

¼ teaspoon salt

4-ounces bacon, cut into tiny pieces

Directions:

Slice bacon into tiny pieces and sprinkle it with cayenne pepper, salt, and paprika. Mix the chopped bacon. Spread butter on the bottom of ramekin dishes and beat the eggs there. Add the chives and shredded cheese. Add the chopped bacon over egg mixture in ramekin dishes. Place the ramekins in your air fryer basket. Preheat your air fryer to 360°Fahrenheit. Place the air fryer basket in your air fryer and cook for 12-minutes. When the cook time is completed, remove the ramekins from the air fryer and serve warm.

Nutrition:

Calories 553 Fat 43.3g Carbs 2.3g Protein 37.3g

5. Breakfast Hash

Preparation Time: 10 minutes

Cooking Time: 8 minutes

Servings: 4

Ingredients:

7-ounces bacon, cooked

1 zucchini, cubed into small pieces

4-ounces cheddar cheese, shredded

2 tablespoons butter

1 teaspoon ground thyme

1 teaspoon cilantro

1 teaspoon paprika

1 teaspoon ground black pepper

1 teaspoon salt

Directions:

Chop the zucchini into small cubes and sprinkle with ground

black pepper, salt, paprika, cilantro and ground thyme.

Preheat your air fryer to 400°Fahrenheit. Add butter to the air fryer basket tray. Melt the butter and add the zucchini cubes.

Cook the zucchini cubes for 5-minutes. Meanwhile, shred the cheddar cheese. Add the bacon to the zucchini cubes. Sprinkle the zucchini mixture with shredded cheese and cook for 3-minutes more. When cooking is completed, transfer the breakfast hash into serving bowls.

Nutrition:

Calories 445

Fat 36.1g

Carbs 3.5g

Protein 26.3g

6. Sweet Strawberries Pancake

Preparation Time: 14 minutes

Cooking Time: 16 minutes

Servings: 4

Ingredients:

3 eggs, beaten

2 tbsp unsalted butter

½ cup flour

2 tbsp sugar, powdered

½ cup milk

1½ cups fresh strawberries, sliced

Directions:

Preheat your Air Fryer to 330 F. Add butter to a pan and melt over low heat. In a bowl, mix flour, milk, eggs and vanilla until fully incorporated. Add the mixture to the pan with melted butter. Place the pan in your air fryer's cooking basket and cook for 12-16 minutes until the pancake is fluffy and golden brown. Drizzle powdered sugar and toss sliced strawberries on top.

Nutrition:

Calories 342.8

Fat 7.9g

Carbs 55.8g

Protein 11.4g

7. Creamy Parmesan & Ham Shirred Eggs

Preparation Time: 5 minutes

Cooking Time: 15 minutes

Servings: 2

Ingredients:

2 tsp. butter, for greasing

4 eggs, divided

2 tbsp. heavy cream

4 slices of ham

3 tbsp. parmesan cheese

¼ tsp. paprika

¾ tsp. salt

¼ tsp. pepper

2 tsp. chopped chives

Directions:

Preheat the air fryer to 320 F. Grease a pie pan with the butter.

Arrange the ham slices on the bottom of the pan to cover it

completely. Whisk one egg along with the heavy cream, salt and pepper, in a small bowl.

Pour the mixture over the ham slices. Crack the other eggs over the ham. Sprinkle with Parmesan cheese. Cook for 14 minutes. Season with paprika, garnish with chives and serve with bread.

Nutrition:

Calories 136.2

Fat 7.2g

Carbs 1.1g

Protein 16.2g

CHAPTER 2

Mains

8. Taco Meatballs

Preparation Time: 5 minutes

Cooking Time: 10 minutes

Servings: 4

Ingredients:

For the Meatballs

1 pound 85% lean ground beef

½ cup shredded Mexican cheese blend

1 large egg

¼ cup finely minced onion

¼ cup chopped fresh cilantro

3 cloves garlic, minced

2½ tablespoons taco seasoning

1 teaspoon kosher salt

1 teaspoon black pepper

For the Sauce

¼ cup sour cream

½ cup salsa

1 to 2 teaspoons Cholula hot sauce or Sriracha

Directions:

For the meatballs: In the bowl of a stand mixer fitted with the paddle attachment, combine the ground beef, cheese, egg, onion, cilantro, garlic, taco seasoning, salt, and pepper. Mix on low speed until all of the ingredients are incorporated, 2 to 3 minutes.

Form the mixture into 12 meatballs and arrange in a single layer in the air fryer basket. Set the air fryer to 400°F for 10 minutes. Use a meat thermometer to ensure the meatballs have reached an internal temperature of 160°F (for medium).

Meanwhile, for the sauce: In a small bowl, combine the sour

cream, salsa, and hot sauce. Stir until well combined. Transfer

the meatballs to a serving bowl. Ladle the sauce over the

meatballs and serve.

Nutrition:

Calories 315

Fat 18.9g

Carbs 12.9

Protein 23.5

9.　Wonton Meatballs

Preparation Time: 15 minutes

Cooking Time:　25 minutes

Servings:　4

Ingredients:

1pound ground pork

2 large eggs

¼ cup chopped green onions (white and green parts)

¼ cup chopped fresh cilantro or parsley

1 tablespoon minced fresh ginger

3 cloves garlic, minced

2 teaspoons soy sauce

1 teaspoon oyster sauce

½ teaspoon kosher salt 1 teaspoon black pepper

Directions:

In the bowl of a stand mixer fitted with the paddle attachment,

combine the pork, eggs, green onions, cilantro, ginger, garlic, soy sauce, oyster sauce, salt, and pepper. Mix on low speed until all of the ingredients are incorporated, 2 to 3 minutes. Form the mixture into 12 meatballs and arrange in a single layer in the air fryer basket.

Set the air fryer to 350°F for 10 minutes. Use a meat thermometer to ensure the meatballs have reached an internal temperature of 145°F. Transfer the meatballs to a bowl and serve.

Nutrition:

Calories 243

Fat 12g

Carbs 25g

Protein 10.3g

10.   Swedish Meatballs

Preparation Time: 5 minutes

Cooking Time: 10 minutes

Servings: 5

Ingredients:

For the meatballs

1 pound 93% lean ground beef

1 (1-ounce) packet Lipton Onion Recipe Soup & Dip Mix

⅓ cup bread crumbs

1 egg, beaten

Salt

Pepper

For the gravy 1 cup beef broth

⅓ cup heavy cream 3 tablespoons all-purpose flour

Directions:

In a large bowl, combine the ground beef, onion soup mix, bread crumbs, egg, and salt and pepper to taste. Mix thoroughly. Using 2 tablespoons of the meat mixture, create each meatball by rolling the beef mixture around in your hands.

This should yield about 10 meatballs. Place the meatballs in the Air fryer. It is okay to stack them. Cook for 14 minutes. While the meatballs cook,

Prepare the gravy. Heat a saucepan over medium-high heat. Add the beef broth and heavy cream. Stir for 1 to 2 minutes. Add the flour and stir. Cover and allow the sauce to simmer for 3 to 4 minutes, or until thick. Drizzle the gravy over the meatballs and serve.

Nutrition:

Calories 342.3

Fat 23g

Carbs 15g

Protein 12.4g

11. Air-Fried Philly Cheesesteak

Preparation: 5 minutesCooking: 21 minutes Servings: 4

Ingredients:

Large hoagie bun, sliced in half

6 ounces of sirloin or flank steak, sliced into bite-sized pieces

½ white onion, rinsed and sliced

½ red pepper, rinsed and sliced

Slices of American cheese

Directions:

Set the air fryer to 320 degrees for 10 minutes. Arrange the steak pieces, onions and peppers on a piece of tin foil, flat and not overlapping, and set the tin foil on one side of the air-fryer basket. The foil should not take up more than half of the surface; the juices from the steak and the moisture from the vegetables will mingle while cooking. Lay the hoagie-bun halves, crusty-side up and soft-side down, on the other half of the air-fryer.

After 10 minutes, the air fryer will shut off; the hoagie buns should be starting to crisp and the steak and vegetables will have begun to cook. Carefully, flip the hoagie buns so they are now crusty-side down and soft-side up; cover both sides with one slice each of American cheese. With a long spoon, gently stir the steak, onions and peppers in the foil to ensure even coverage. Set the air fryer to 360 degrees for 6 minutes. After 6 minutes, when the fryer shuts off, the cheese will be perfectly melted over the toasted bread, and the steak will be juicy on the inside and crispy on the outside. Remove the cheesy hoagie halves first, using tongs, and set on a serving plate; then cover one side with the steak, and top with the onions and peppers. Close with the other cheesy hoagie-half, slice into two pieces, and enjoy.

Nutrition:

Calories 740 Fat 36g Carbs 58g Protein 49g

12. Montreal Steak Burgers

Preparation: 10 minutesCooking: 20 minutes Servings: 4

Ingredients:

1 teaspoon mustard seeds

1 teaspoon cumin seeds

1 teaspoon coriander seeds

1 teaspoon dried minced garlic

1 teaspoon dried red pepper flakes

1 teaspoon kosher salt

2 teaspoons black peppercorns

1 pound 85% lean ground beef

2 tablespoons Worcestershire sauce

4 hamburger buns

Mayonnaise

Directions:

In a mortar and pestle, combine the mustard seeds, cumin seeds, coriander seeds, dried garlic, pepper flakes, salt, and peppercorns. Roughly crush the seeds, stopping before you make a fine powder. In a large bowl, combine the spice mixture with the ground beef and Worcestershire sauce. Gently mix until well combined. Divide the meat into four portions and form into round patties. Make a slight depression in the middle of each patty with your thumb to prevent them from puffing up into a dome shape while cooking.

Place the patties in the air fryer basket. Set the air fryer to 350°F for 10 minutes. Use a meat thermometer to ensure the burgers have reached an internal temperature of 160°F (for medium). To serve, place the burgers on the buns and top with mayonnaise.

Nutrition:

Calories 650 Fat 40g Carbs 47g

Protein 25g

13.   Chickpea Soft Tacos

Preparation: 10 minutesCooking: 12 minutesServings: 4

Ingredients:

1 small onion, chopped 1 red bell pepper, sliced

1 tablespoon olive oil

1 (15-ounce) can chickpeas, drained and rinsed

1 chipotle in adobo sauce, minced 1 tablespoon adobo sauce

2 tablespoons freshly squeezed lime juice

1 teaspoon chili powder

½ teaspoon cumin

½ teaspoon sea salt

4 (6-inch) corn tortillas

1 avocado, cubed

Directions:

In a 6-inch metal bowl, combine the onion and bell pepper. Drizzle with the olive oil and toss to coat. Put the bowl in the air fryer basket.

Set or preheat the air fryer to 375°F and roast for 2 to 4 minutes or until the vegetables are crisp-tender.

Remove the bowl and stir in the chickpeas, chipotle, adobo sauce, lime juice, chili powder, cumin, and salt.

Return the bowl to the air fryer and roast for 7 to 8 minutes, stirring once halfway through cooking time, until the ingredients are hot.

Fill the tortillas with the chickpea filling and avocado and serve.

Nutrition:

Calories 316

Protein 9g

Fat 16g

Saturated Fat 3g

Carbs 39g

Sodium 482g

Fiber 11g

14.   Falafel in Pita

Preparation Time: 15 minutes

Cooking Time:18 minutes

Servings:4

Ingredients:

1 (15-ounce) can chickpeas, drained and rinsed

¼ cup ground almonds

¼ cup chopped flat-leaf parsley

2 tablespoons chopped fresh cilantro

2 tablespoons freshly squeezed lemon juice

1 tablespoon peanut butter

1 scallion, thinly sliced

2 garlic cloves, chopped

½ teaspoon sea salt

⅛ Teaspoon freshly ground black pepper

½ cup almond flour

Cooking oil spray

2 pita breads, cut in half and split open

1 cup halved cherry tomatoes

1 cup sliced seeded cucumber

⅓ Cup plain Greek yogurt

Directions:

In a blender or food processor, combine the chickpeas, almonds, parsley, cilantro, lemon juice, peanut butter, scallion, garlic, salt, and pepper and blend or pulse until the mixture is ground and combined but is not mushy.

Place the almond flour in a shallow bowl.

Using wet hands to prevent sticking, form the chickpea mixture into 2-inch balls. Roll the balls in the almond flour and place in the air fryer basket in a single layer. Spray the tops of the falafel with cooking oil. You may have to cook the falafel in two batches.

Set or preheat the air fryer to 375°F. Fry the falafel for 14 to 18 minutes, turning once during cooking time and spraying with more oil, until they are crisp and hot.

Make the falafel into sandwiches by placing a few balls each into the pita bread halves with the tomatoes, cucumber, and yogurt. Serve.

Nutrition:

Calories 241

Protein 12g

Fat 11g

Saturated Fat 1g

Carbs 27g

Sugar 7g

Sodium 277g

Fiber 8g

CHAPTER 3

Sides

15.   Cheesy Breaded Mushrooms

Preparation Time: 10 minutes

Cooking Time: 7 minutes

Servings: 2

Ingredients:

8 ¾ oz. Button mushrooms

1 Egg

Salt and Pepper

Flour

Breadcrumbs

3 oz Parmigiano cheese 3 oz

Directions:

Mix together the cheese and breadcrumbs in a bowl. Whisk the egg in another bowl. Dredge the mushrooms in flour, dip in egg and then coat with the breadcrumb mix. Cook for 7 minutes in an air fryer at 360 degrees Fahrenheit, tossing once in between.

Nutrition:

Calories 156.2g Fat 12g Protein 10.9g

16.   Spanish Style Spiced Potatoes

Preparation Time: 10 minutes

Cooking Time: 23 minutes Servings: 4

Ingredients:

3 Potatoes

1 Onion

½ cup Tomato sauce

1 Tomato

1 tablespoon Red wine vinegar

2 tablespoon Olive oil

1 teaspoon Paprika

1 teaspoon Chili powder

2 teaspoon Coriander

2 teaspoon Thyme

1 teaspoon Mixed spice

1 teaspoon Oregano

1 teaspoon Rosemary

Salt and pepper

Directions:

Toss the chips in olive oil and cook in an air fryer for 15 minutes at 360 degrees Fahrenheit. Combine the rest of the Ingredients: in a baking dish and mix well. Place the sauce in the air fryer for 8 minutes. Toss the potatoes in the sauce and serve.

Nutrition: Calories 342 Fat 23g Protein 8g

17. Parmesan Zucchini Rounds

Preparation Time: 25 minutes

Cooking Time: 10 minutes

Servings: 4

Ingredients:

4 zucchinis; sliced

1 ½ cups parmesan; grated

¼ cup parsley; chopped.

1 egg; whisked

1 egg white; whisked

½ tsp. garlic powder

Cooking spray

Directions:

Take a bowl and mix the egg with egg whites, parmesan, parsley and garlic powder and whisk. Dredge each zucchini slice in this mix, place them all in your air fryer's basket, grease them with cooking spray and cook at 370°F for 20 minutes.

Divide between plates and serve as a side dish.

Nutrition:

Calories183

Fat 6g

Carbs 3g

Protein 8g

18.   Green Bean Casserole

Preparation Time: 25 minutes

Cooking Time: 10 minutes

Servings: 4

Ingredients:

1 lb. fresh green beans

½ oz. pork rinds

1 oz. full-fat cream cheese

½ cup heavy whipping cream.

¼ cup diced yellow onion

½ cup chopped white mushrooms

½ cup chicken broth

4 tbsp. unsalted butter.

¼ tsp. xanthan gum

Directions:

In a medium skillet over medium heat, melt the butter. Sauté the onion and mushrooms until they become soft and fragrant, about 3–5 minutes. Add the heavy whipping cream, cream cheese and broth to the pan. Whisk until smooth. Bring to a boil and then reduce to a simmer. Sprinkle the xanthan gum into the pan and remove from heat. Chop the green beans into 2-inch pieces and place into a 4-cup round baking dish. Pour the sauce mixture over them and stir until coated. Top the dish with ground pork rinds. Place into the air fryer basket. Adjust the temperature to 320 Degrees F and set the timer for 15 minutes. Top will be golden and green beans fork tender when fully cooked. Serve warm.

Nutrition:

Calories 267

Protein 3.6g

Fat 23.4g

Carbs 9.7g

19.   Cilantro Roasted Cauliflower

Preparation Time: 17 minutes

Cooking Time: 7 minutes

Servings: 4

Ingredients:

2 cups chopped cauliflower florets

1 medium lime

2 tbsp. chopped cilantro

2 tbsp. coconut oil; melted

½ tsp. garlic powder

2 tsp. chili powder

Directions:

Take a large bowl, toss cauliflower with coconut oil. Sprinkle it with chili powder and garlic powder. Place seasoned cauliflower into the air fryer basket. Adjust the temperature to 350 Degrees F and set the timer for 7 minutes. Cauliflower will be tender and begin to turn golden at the edges. Place into a serving bowl. Cut the lime into quarters and squeeze juice over cauliflower. Garnish with cilantro.

Nutrition:

Calories 73

Protein 1.1

Fat 6.5g

Carbs 3.3g

20. Easy Home Fries

Preparation Time: 20 minutes

Cooking Time: 10 minutes

 Servings: 4

Ingredients:

½ medium white onions

1 medium green bell pepper

1 medium jicama

1 tbsp. coconut oil

½ tsp. pink Himalayan salt

¼ tsp. ground black pepper

Directions:

Cut jicama into 1-inch cubes. Place into a large bowl and toss with coconut oil until coated. Sprinkle it with pepper and salt.

 Place into the air fryer basket with peppers and onion. Adjust the temperature to 400 Degrees F and set the timer for 10 minutes.

Shake two or three times during cooking. Jicama will be tender and dark around the edges. Serve immediately.

Nutrition:

Calories 97

Protein1.5g

Fat 3.3g

Carbs 15.8g

21.   Healthy Garlic Stuffed Mushrooms

Preparation Time: 25 minutes

Cooking Time: 10 minutes

Servings: 3

Ingredients:

6 mushrooms

1 ounce. onion

1 tablespoon breadcrumbs

1 tablespoon oil

1 teaspoon garlic

1 teaspoon parsley

salt to taste

pepper to taste

Directions:

Mix breadcrumbs, oil, onion, parsley, salt, pepper and garlic in a medium sized bowl. Remove middle stalks from mushrooms and fill them with crumb mixture. Cook in an Air

Fryer for 10 minutes at 350 - degrees Fahrenheit. Serve with mayo dip and enjoy the right combination.

Nutrition:

Calories 345

Fat 3g

Protein 23g

22. Zucchini and Peppers with Saucy Sweet Potatoes

Preparation Time: 20 minutes

Cooking Time: 15 minutes

Servings: 4

Ingredients:

2 large-sized sweet potatoes

1 medium-sized zucchini

1 Serrano pepper

1 bell pepper 1 2 carrots

1/4 cup olive oil 1 ½ tablespoon maple syrup

1/2 teaspoon porcini powder

1/4 teaspoon mustard powder

1/2 teaspoon fennel seeds

1 tablespoon garlic powder

1/2 teaspoon fine sea salt

1/4 teaspoon ground black pepper

Tomato ketchup; to serve

Directions:

Place the sweet potatoes, zucchini, peppers, and the carrot into the Air Fryer cooking basket. Drizzle with olive oil and toss to coat, cook in the preheated machine at 350 - degrees Fahrenheit for 15 minutes.

While the vegetables are cooking; Preparation Time:are the sauce by thoroughly whisking the other Ingredients:, without the tomato ketchup. Lightly grease a baking dish that fits into your machine.

Transfer cooked vegetables to the baking dish add the sauce and toss to coat well. Turn the machine to 390 - degrees Fahrenheit and cook the vegetables for 5 more minutes. Serve warm with tomato ketchup on the side.

Nutrition:

Calories 234g Fat 4g Protein 5g

23. Rice and Meatball Stuffed Bell Peppers

Preparation Time: 13 minutes

Cooking Time:11 to 17 minutes

Servings:4

Ingredients:

4 bell peppers

1 tablespoon olive oil

1 small onion, chopped

2 cloves garlic, minced

1 cup frozen cooked rice, thawed

16 to 20 small frozen precooked meatballs, thawed

½ cup tomato sauce

2 tablespoons Dijon mustard

Directions:

To prepare the peppers, cut off about ½ inch of the tops.

Carefully remove the membranes and seeds from inside the

peppers. Set aside.

In a 6-by-6-by-2-inch pan, combine the olive oil, onion, and garlic. Bake in the air fryer for 2 to 4 minutes or until crisp and tender. Remove the vegetable mixture from the pan and set aside in a medium bowl.

Add the rice, meatballs, tomato sauce, and mustard to the vegetable mixture and stir to combine.

Stuff the peppers with the meat-vegetable mixture.

Place the peppers in the air fryer basket and bake for 9 to 13 minutes or until the filling is hot and the peppers are tender.

Nutrition:

Calories 487 Total Fat 21g

Saturated Fat 7g

Cholesterol 47mg

Sodium 797mg

Carbs 57g

Fiber 6g

Protein 26g

CHAPTER 4

Fish and Seafood

24. Simple Salmon

Preparation Time: 22 minutes

Cooking Time: 12 minutes

Servings: 2

Ingredients:

2 (4-oz. salmon fillets, skin removed

1 medium lemon 2 tbsp. unsalted butter; melted

½ tsp. dried dill ½ tsp. garlic powder

Directions:

Place each fillet on a 5" × 5" square of aluminum foil. Drizzle

with butter and sprinkle with garlic powder.

Zest half of the lemon and sprinkle zest over salmon. Slice other half of the lemon and lay two slices on each piece of salmon. Sprinkle dill over salmon

Gather and fold foil at the top and sides to fully close packets. Place foil packets into the air fryer basket. Adjust the temperature to 400 Degrees F and set the timer for 12 minutes

Salmon will be easily flaked and have an internal temperature of at least 145 Degrees F when fully cooked.

Nutrition:

Calories: 252Protein: 29g

Fiber: 4g Fat: 15g

Carbs: 2g

25. Cajun Spiced Salmon

Preparation Time: 10 minutes

Cooking Time: 8 minutes

Servings: 8

Ingredients:

4 tablespoons Cajun seasoning

4 salmon steaks

Directions:

Add Cajun seasoning in a bowl and rub salmon evenly with it.

Preheat the air fryer to 385 degrees F.

Arrange air fryer grill pan and place salmon steaks on it.

Cook for about 8 minutes and flip once in the middle way.

Take out and serve hot.

Tip: Set aside salmon steaks for at least 15 minutes before placing them in the air fryer.

Nutrition:

Calories 118 Total Fat 5.5g Total Carbs 0g

26.   Tangy Salmon

Preparation Time: 10 minutes Cooking Time: 7 minutes

Servings: 8

Ingredients:

4 tablespoons Cajun seasoning

8 salmon fillets

4 tablespoons fresh lemon juice

Directions:

Season salmon fillets with Cajun seasoning and set aside for 15 minutes. Preheat the air fryer to 360 degrees F and arrange grill pan in it. Place salmon fillets on the grill pan and cook for about 7 minutes. Drizzle with lemon juice and serve.

Tip: Salmon fillets should be ¾-inch thick

Nutrition:

Calories 237 Total Fat 11.1g

Total Carbs 0.2g

Protein 34.7g

27. Sesame Seeds Coated Fish

Preparation Time: 20 minutes

Cooking Time: 14 minutes

Servings: 28

Ingredients:

½ cup sesame seeds, toasted

½ teaspoon dried rosemary, crushed

8 tablespoons olive oil

14 frozen fish fillets (white fish of your choice)

6 eggs

½ cup breadcrumbs

8 tablespoons plain flour

Salt and freshly ground black pepper, to taste

Directions:

Take three dishes, place flour in one, crack eggs in the other

and mix remaining ingredients except fillets in the third one.

Now, coat fillets in the flour and dip in the beaten eggs.

Then, dredge generously with the sesame seeds mixture.

Meanwhile, preheat the air fryer to 390 degrees F and line the air fryer basket with the foil.

Arrange fillets in the basket and cook for about 14 minutes, flipping once in the middle way.

Take out and serve hot.

Tip: Use shallow dishes.

Nutrition:

Calories 179 Fat 9.3g

Carbs 15.8g Sugar 0.7g

Fiber 1g Protein 7.7g

28.   Sweet & Sour Glazed Salmon

Preparation Time: 12 minutes

Cooking Time: 20 minutes

Servings: 2

Ingredients:

1/3 cup soy sauce

1/3 cup honey

3 tsp rice wine vinegar

1 tsp water

4 oz.salmon fillets

Directions:

In a small shallow container, mix the soy sauce, honey, vinegar, and water. In another small bowl, reserve about half of the mixture. Add salmon fillets in the remaining mixture and coat well.

Cover the bowl and refrigerate to marinate for about 2 hours.

Press the "Power Button" of Air Fry Oven and turn the dial to select the "Air Fry" mode.

Press the Time button and again turn the dial to set the cooking time to 12 minutes. Now push the Temp button and rotate the dial to set the temperature at 355 degrees F. Press the "Start/Pause" button to start.

When the unit beeps to show that it is preheated, open the lid. Arrange the salmon fillets in greased "Air Fry Basket" and insert them in the oven. Flip the salmon fillets once halfway through and coat with the reserved marinade after every 3 minutes. Serve hot.

Nutrition:

Calories 462

Fat 12.3 g

Carbs 49.8 g

Protein 41.3 g

CHAPTER 5

Poultry

29. BBQ Chicken Wings

Preparation Time: 20 minutes

Cooking Time: 25 minutes

Servings: 4

Ingredients:

2 pounds chicken wingettes and drumettes

1/2 cup ketchup

3 tablespoons white vinegar

2 tablespoons honey

2 tablespoons molasses

1/2 teaspoon liquid smoke

1/4 teaspoon paprika

1/4 teaspoon garlic powder

Pinch of cayenne pepper

Directions:

Arrange the wings onto 2 cooking trays in a single layer.

Arrange the drip pan in the bottom of Kalorik Maxx Plus Air fryer oven cooking chamber.

Select Air fryer oven and then adjust the temperature to 380 degrees F.

Set the timer for 25 minutes and press the Start.

When the display shows Add Food insert 1 tray in the top position and another in the bottom position.

When the display shows Turn Food do not turn the food but switch the position of cooking trays.

Meanwhile, in a small pan, add the remaining ingredients over medium heat and cook for about 10 minutes, stirring occasionally.

When cooking is complete, remove the trays from Oven.

In a large bowl, add the chicken wings and honey mixture and toss to coat well.

Serve immediately.

Nutrition:

Calories 524

Fat 16.9g Carbs 24g

Protein 66.2g

30. Simple Turkey Breast

Preparation Time: 10 minutes

Cooking Time: 45 minutes

Servings: 8

Ingredients:

1 turkey breast

Salt and ground black pepper

Directions:

Season the turkey breast with salt and black pepper evenly.

With kitchen twines, tie the turkey breast to keep it compact. Arrange the turkey breast in the rotisserie basket and attach the lid.

Arrange the drip pan in the bottom of Kalorik Maxx Plus Air fryer oven cooking chamber. Select Air fryer oven and then adjust the temperature to 360 degrees F. Set the timer for 45 minutes and press the Start.

Then, Then, close the door and touch Rotate.When the display shows Add Food arrange the rotisserie basket, on the rotisserie spit. Then, close the door and touch Rotate.

When cooking is complete, press the red lever to release the rod. Remove from the Oven and place the turkey breast onto a platter for about 5-10 minutes before slicing. With a sharp knife, cut the turkey breast into desired sized slices and serve.

Nutrition:

Calories 153

Fat 1.5g

Carbs 3g

Protein 31.9g

31.   565.Herbed Turkey Breast

Preparation Time: 15 minutes

Cooking Time: 1 hour

Servings: 8

Ingredients:

2 tablespoons olive oil

2 tablespoons lemon juice

1 tablespoon garlic, minced

2 teaspoons ground mustard

Salt and ground black pepper

1 teaspoon ground sage

1 teaspoon dried thyme

1 teaspoon dried rosemary

1 turkey breast

Directions:

In a small bowl, add all the ingredients except the turkey

breast and mix until well combined.

Rub the oil mixture on the outside of the turkey breast and under any loose skin generously.

Arrange the turkey breast onto a cooking tray, skin side up.

Arrange the drip pan in the bottom of Kalorik Maxx Plus Air fryer oven cooking chamber.

Select Air fryer oven and then adjust the temperature to 360 degrees F.

Set the timer for 60 minutes and press the Start.

When the display shows Add Food insert the cooking tray in the center position.

When cooking is complete, press the red lever to release the rod.

Remove from the Oven and place the turkey breast onto a platter for about 5-10 minutes before slicing.

With a sharp knife, cut the turkey breast into desired sized

Nutrition: Calories 214 Fat 6.6g Carbs 8.1g Protein 29.4g

CHAPTER 6

Meat

32.   Chinese Salt and Pepper Pork Chop Stir-fry

Preparation Time: 10 minutes

Cooking Time: 15 minutes

Servings: 4

Ingredients:

Pork Chops:

olive oil

¾cup almond flour

¼ tsp. pepper

½ tsp. salt

1 egg white

Pork Chops

Stir-fry:

¼ tsp. pepper

1 tsp. sea salt

2 tbsp. olive oil

2 sliced scallions

2 sliced jalapeno peppers

Directions:

Coat the air fryer basket with olive oil. Whisk pepper, salt, and egg white together till foamy. Cut pork chops into pieces, leaving just a bit on bones. Pat dry. Add pieces of pork to egg white mixture, coating well. Let sit for 20 minutes. Put marinated chops into a large bowl and add almond flour. Dredge and shake off excess and place into an air fryer. Set temperature to 360°F, and set time to 12 minutes. Cook for 12 minutes at 360 degrees. Turn up the heat to 400 degrees and cook for another 6 minutes till pork chops are nice and crisp. To make stir-fry, remove jalapeno seeds and chop up. Chop scallions and mix with jalapeno pieces. Heat a skillet with olive oil.

Stir-fry pepper, salt, scallions, and jalapenos 60 seconds. Then add fried pork pieces to skills and toss with scallion mixture. Stir-fry 1-2 minutes till well coated and hot.

Nutrition:

Calories 294

Fat 17g

Protein 36g

33.   Garlic Putter Pork Chops

Preparation Time: 5 minutes

Cooking Time: 10 minutes Servings: 4

Ingredients:

2 tsp. parsley   2 tsp. grated garlic cloves

1 tbsp. coconut oil   1 tbsp. coconut butter   4 pork chops

Directions:

Ensure your air fryer is preheated to 350 degrees. Mix butter, coconut oil, and all seasoning together. Then rub seasoning mixture over all sides of pork chops. Place in foil, seal, and chill for 1 hour. Remove pork chops from foil and place into an air fryer. Set temperature to 350°F, and set time to 7 minutes. Cook 7 minutes on one side and 8 minutes on the other. Drizzle with olive oil and serve alongside a green salad.

Nutrition:

Calories 526 Fat 23g Protein 41g

34. Roasted Pork Chops with Mushrooms

Preparation Time: 10 minutes

Cooking Time: 25 minutes

Servings: 4

Ingredients:

1 lb. boneless pork chops

2 carrots, cut into sticks

1 cup mushrooms, sliced

2 tbsp. olive oil

2 garlic cloves, minced

1 tsp. cayenne pepper

1 tsp. dried oregano

1 tsp. dried thyme

salt and black pepper to taste

Directions:

Preheat air fryer to 360 F. Season the chops with cayenne pepper, oregano, thyme, salt, and pepper. In a bowl, combine carrots, olive oil, mushrooms, and salt. Place the veggies in a greased baking dish and then in the air fryer basket. Top with pork chops and Bake for 15-18 minutes, shaking once.

Nutrition:

Calories 734

Fat 56g

Protein 32g

35. Baby Back Pork Ribs with BBQ Sauce

Preparation Time: 10 minutes

Cooking Time: 25 minutes Servings: 4

Ingredients:

1 tbsp. smoked paprika

1 tsp. cayenne pepper

1 rack baby back pork ribs, cut into individual pieces

1 tsp. onion powder

1 tsp. garlic powder

1 tsp. pomegranate molasses

½ tsp. oregano

½ cup barbecue sauce

salt and black pepper to taste

2 scallions, chopped

Directions:

In a bowl, combine paprika, cayenne pepper, garlic powder,

pomegranate molasses, onion powder, oregano, salt, and

pepper. Add in the ribs and toss to coat. Cover and let in the fridge for 30 minutes. Preheat the air fryer to 360 F. Spray ribs with cooking spray and place in the fryer basket. Cook for 15-18 minutes, flipping once halfway through. Drizzle with barbecue sauce, scatter scallions over, and serve.

Nutrition:

Calories 823

Fat 52g

Protein 33g

36.   Crispy Pork Chops

Preparation Time: 10 minutes

Cooking Time: 20 minutes Servings: 4

Ingredients:

4 boneless pork chops

salt and black pepper to taste

1 cup tbsp. crushed pork rinds

¼ tsp. garlic powder

¼ tsp. onion powder

1 tsp. paprika

2 eggs

4 small slices cold butter

Directions:

Preheat the Air fryer to 390 F. Spray the air fryer basket with cooking spray. In a bowl, combine pork rinds, garlic and onion powders, paprika, salt, and pepper and mix well. In another bowl, whisk the eggs with salt. Dip the pork first in the eggs and then coat with the pork rind mixture. Spray with cooking spray and place in the air fryer basket. Air Fry for 15 minutes, flipping once halfway through. Remove to a serving plate and top with butter slices to serve.

Nutrition:

Calories 586 Fat 53g

Protein 48g

CHAPTER 7

Vegetables

37.   Herbed Vegetable Mélange

Preparation Time: 10 minutes

Cooking Time: 18 minutes

Servings: 4

Ingredients:

1 red bell pepper, sliced

1 (8 oz.) package sliced mushrooms

1 yellow summer squash, sliced

3 cloves garlic, sliced

1 tbsp. olive oil

½ tsp. dried thyme

½ tsp. dried basil

½ tsp. dried tarragon

Directions:

Place the pepper, mushrooms, squash, and garlic in a medium bowl and drizzle with the olive oil. Toss, add the thyme, basil, and tarragon, and toss again. Place the vegetables in the air fryer basket. Roast for 14 to 18 minutes or until the vegetables are tender. Air Fryer tip: When you add dried herbs to an air fryer recipe, whether you're making roasted vegetables or chicken, they must stick to the food or they will just blow around the air fryer and may burn. Always coat veggies or meat with a little oil before you add herbs, then they will stay on the food and flavor it.

Nutrition:

Calories 63

Fat 4g

Protein 3g

38.   Steamed Green Veggie Trio

Preparation Time: 6 minutes

Cooking Time: 9 minutes

Servings: 4

Ingredients:

2 cups broccoli florets

1 cup green beans

1 tbsp. olive oil

1 tbsp. lemon juice

1 cup frozen baby peas

2 tbsp. honey mustard

pinch salt

freshly ground black pepper

Directions:

Put the broccoli and green beans in the basket of the air fryer.

Put 2 tablespoons of water in the air fryer pan. Sprinkle the

vegetables with the olive oil and lemon juice, and toss. Steam for 6 minutes, then remove the basket from the air fryer and

add the peas. Steam for 3 minutes or until the vegetables are

hot and tender. Transfer the vegetables to a serving dish and

drizzle with the honey mustard and sprinkle with salt and

pepper. Toss and serve.

Nutrition:

Calories 99

Fat 4g

Protein 4g

39.   Garlic and Sesame Carrots

Cooking Time: 16 minutes

Servings: 4

Ingredients:

1 lb. baby carrots

1 tbsp. sesame oil

½ tsp.dried dill

pinch salt

freshly ground black pepper

6 cloves garlic, peeled

3 tbsp. sesame seeds

Directions:

Place the baby carrots in a medium bowl. Drizzle with sesame oil, add the dill, salt, and pepper, and toss to coat well. Place the carrots in the basket of the air fryer. Roast for 8 minutes, shaking the basket once during cooking time. Add the garlic to the air fryer. Roast for 8 minutes, shaking the basket once during cooking time, or until the garlic and carrots are lightly browned. Transfer to a serving bowl and sprinkle with the sesame seeds before serving.

Nutrition:

Calories 116 Fat 7g Protein 2g

40. Roasted Bell Peppers with Garlic

Preparation Time: 8 minutes

Cooking Time: 22 minutes

Servings: 4

Ingredients:

1 red bell pepper

1 yellow bell pepper

1 orange bell pepper

1 green bell pepper

2 tbsp. olive oil, divided

½ tsp. dried marjoram

pinch salt

freshly ground black pepper

1 head garlic

Directions:

Slice the bell peppers into 1-inch strips. In a large bowl, toss

the bell peppers with 1 tablespoon of the oil. Sprinkle on the marjoram, salt, and pepper, and toss again. Cut off the top of the garlic head and place the cloves on an oiled square of aluminum foil. Drizzle with the remaining olive oil.

Wrap the garlic in the foil. Place the wrapped garlic in the air fryer and roast for 15 minutes, then add the bell peppers. Roast for 7 minutes or until the peppers are tender and the garlic is soft. Transfer the peppers to a serving dish. Remove the garlic from the air fryer and unwrap the foil. When cool enough to handle, squeeze the garlic cloves out of the papery skin and mix with the bell peppers.

Nutrition:

Calories 108

Fat 7g

Protein 2g

CHAPTER 8

Soup and Stews

41.   Mexican Beef Soup

Preparation Time: 30 minutes

Cooking Time: 25 minutes

Servings: 4

Ingredients:

1-pound beef stew meat

3/4-pound potatoes cut into 3/4-inch cubes

2 cups frozen corn, thawed

2 medium carrots, cut into 1/2-inch slices

1 medium onion, chopped

2 garlic cloves, minced

1-1/2 tsp. dried oregano

1 tsp. ground cumin

1/2 tsp. salt

1/4 tsp. crushed red pepper flakes

2 cups beef stock

1 can diced tomatoes and green chilies

Directions:

In a baking dish that fits your air fryer oven, mix the turkey with the rest of the ingredients except the parsley, toss, introduce the dish in the fryer, bake at 380°F for 25 minutes

Divide into bowls, sprinkle the parsley on top and serve.

Nutrition:

Calories 250

Fat 11g

Fiber 2g

Carbs 6g

Protein 12g

CHAPTER 9

Snacks

42.   Sunflower Seed Bread

Preparation Time: 15 minutes

Cooking Time: 18 minutes

Servings: 6

Ingredients:

2/3 cup whole-wheat flour

2/3 cup plain flour

1/3 cup sunflower seeds

½ sachet instant yeast

1 teaspoon salt

2/3-1 cup lukewarm water

Directions:

In a bowl, mix together the flours, sunflower seeds, yeast, and salt.

Slowly, add in the water, stirring continuously until a soft dough ball forms.

Now, move the dough onto a lightly floured surface and knead for about 5 minutes using your hands.

Make a ball from the dough and place into a bowl.

With a plastic wrap, cover the bowl and place at a warm place for about 30 minutes.

Grease a cake pan.

Coat the top of dough with water and place into the prepared cake pan.

Press "Power Button" of Air Fry Oven and turn the dial to select the "Air Crisp" mode.

Press the Time button and again turn the dial to set the cooking time to 18 minutes.

Now push the Temp button and rotate the dial to set the temperature at 390 degrees F.

Press "Start/Pause" button to start.

When the unit beeps to show that it is preheated, open the lid.

Arrange the pan in "Air Fry Basket" and insert in the oven.

Place the pan onto a wire rack to cool for about 10 minutes.

Carefully, invert the bread onto wire rack to cool completely before slicing.

Cut the bread into desired-sized slices and serve.

Nutrition:

Calories 132

Total Fat 1.7 g Saturated Fat 0.1 g

Cholesterol 0 mg Sodium 390 mg

Total Carbs 24.4 g

Fiber 1.6 g

Sugar 0.1 g

Protein 4.9 g

43. Date Bread

Preparation Time: 15 minutes

Cooking Time: 22 minutes

Servings: 10

Ingredients:

2½ cup dates, pitted and chopped

¼ cup butter

1 cup hot water

1½ cups flour

½ cup brown sugar

1 teaspoon baking powder

1 teaspoon baking soda

½ teaspoon salt

1 egg

Directions:

In a large bowl, add the dates, butter and top with the hot

water.

Set aside for about 5 minutes.

In another bowl, mix together the flour, brown sugar, baking powder, baking soda, and salt.

In the same bowl of dates, mix well the flour mixture, and egg.

Grease a baking pan.

Place the mixture into the prepared pan.

Press "Power Button" of Air Fry Oven and turn the dial to select the "Air Crisp" mode.

Press the Time button and again turn the dial to set the cooking time to 22 minutes.

Now push the Temp button and rotate the dial to set the temperature at 340 degrees F.

Press "Start/Pause" button to start.

When the unit beeps to show that it is preheated, open the lid.

Arrange the pan in "Air Fry Basket" and insert in the oven.

Place the pan onto a wire rack to cool for about 10 minutes.

Carefully, invert the bread onto wire rack to cool completely before slicing.

Cut the bread into desired-sized slices and serve.

Nutrition:

Calories 269

Total Fat 5.4 g

Saturated Fat 3.1 g

Cholesterol 29 mg

Sodium 285 mg

Total Carbs 55.1 g

Fiber 4.1 g

Sugar 35.3 g

Protein 3.6 g

CHAPTER 10

Desserts

44. Raspberry Muffins

Preparation Time: 30 minutes

Cooking Time: 20 minutes Servings: 8

Ingredients:

¾ cup raspberries

½ cup swerve

¼ cup coconut flour

¼ cup ghee; melted

1 egg

3 tbsp. cream cheese

2 tbsp. almond meal

½ tsp. baking soda

½ tsp. baking powder

1 tsp. cinnamon powder

Cooking spray

Directions:

Take a bowl and mix all the ingredients except the cooking spray and whisk well. Grease a muffin pan that fits the air fryer with the cooking spray

Pour the raspberry mix, put the pan in the machine and cook at 350°F for 20 minutes. Serve the muffins cold

Nutrition:

Calories: 223

Fat: 7g

Fiber: 2g

Carbs: 4g

Protein: 5g

45. Air Fryer Oven Peppermint Lava Cake

Preparation Time: 15 minutes

Cooking Time: 15 minutes Servings: 4

Ingredients:

 2 large eggs

2/3 cups semisweet chocolate chips

1 tsp. peppermint extract

½ cup cubed butter

6 tablespoons all- purpose flour

  2large egg yolks

2 tablespoons crushed peppermint candies (optional)

1 cup confectioners' sugar

Directions:

Preheat air fryer oven to 375F Melt butter and chocolate chips

in microwave safe bowl for 30 seconds and stir until smooth.

Whisk in eggs, egg yolks, confectioners' sugars and extract

until blended. Fold in flout Grease and flour ramekins, pour batter into ramekins but avoid overfilling it

Place ramekins in air fryer oven basket and cook for 10 to 15 minutes until thermometer reads 160F Remove and allow it sit for 5 minutes, sprinkle with crush candies and enjoy.

Nutrition:

Calories 367 Total Fat 19.2 g

Saturated Fat 9.5 g

Cholesterol 124 mg

Sodium 265 mg

Total Carbs 53.6 g

Fiber 2.7 g Sugar 37.8 g Protein 6.4 g

46. Air Fryer Oven Chocolate Cake

Preparation Time: 15 minutes

Cooking Time: 20 minutes

Servings: 4

Ingredients:

3 eggs

1/2 cup sour cream

1 cup flour

2/3 cup sugar

1 stick butter room temperature

1/3 cup cocoa powder

1 teaspoon baking powder

1/2 teaspoon baking soda

2 teaspoons vanilla

Directions:

Preheat Air fryer oven to 320 degrees

Mix ingredients on low heat and pour into oven attachment

Place in Air fryer oven basket and Set timer to 25 minutes

Once timer rings, insert use toothpick to see if cake is done.

Cool cake on a wire rack

Ice with your favorite chocolate frosting

Nutrition:

Calories 300

Total Fat 12 g

Saturated 7.4 g

Cholesterol 31 mg

Sodium 122 mg

Total Carbs 46.7 g

Fiber 2.3 g Sugar 23.3 g

Protein 3.3 g

47.   Two Ingredients Air Fryer Oven Croutons

Preparation: 10 minutes Cooking: 12 minutes Servings: 2

Ingredients:

2 Slices Whole meal Bread

1 Tbsp Olive Oil

Directions:

Chop slices of bread into medium chunks and place in Air fryer oven.

Add olive oil and cook for 8 minutes on a 200c heat.

Serve over soup or as a snack.

Nutrition:

Calories 369

Total Fat 31 gSaturated Fat 19.5 g

Cholesterol 103 mg Sodium 261 mg

Total Carbs 20 g Fiber 0.1 g

Sugar 17.7 g

Protein 5.1 g

48.   Air Fryer Oven Strawberry Cupcakes

Preparation Time: 10 minutes

Cooking Time: 13 minutes

Servings: 4

Ingredients:

100 g Butter100 g Caster Sugar

2 Medium Eggs100 g Self Raising Flour

½ Tsp Vanilla Essence50 g Butter

100 g Icing Sugar½ Tsp Pink Food Coloring

1 Tbsp Whipped Cream

¼ Cup Fresh Strawberries blended

Directions:

Preheat air fryer oven to 170c.

Cream butter and sugar in a large mixing bowl until light and fluffy; add vanilla essence and beat in eggs one at a time (adding little flour after each egg). Then fold in the rest of the flour.

Place them in little bun cases but don't fill the cases too much.

Place cupcakes in air fryer oven and cook for 8 minutes on 170c.

Meanwhile, cream butter and gradually add icing sugar until you have a creamy mixture, then add food coloring, whipped cream and blended strawberries and mix well.

Once the cupcakes are done, use a piping bag to add topping to them in circular motions

Serve and enjoy

Nutrition:

Calories 317g

Total Fat 11.9 g

Carbs 14.8 g

Fiber 1.1 g

Sugar 8.3 g

Protein 5 g

49. Air Fryer Oven Shortbread

Preparation Time: 10 minutes

Cooking Time: 28 minutes

Servings: 8

Ingredients:

Brownie:

250 g Self Raising Flour

175 g Butter

75 g Caster Sugar

30 g Cocoa Powder

Roses Chocolates

2 Tsp Vanilla Essence

Chocolate Chips

Directions:

Place flour, butter and caster sugar in a bowl, rub butter into flour until it resembles breadcrumbs then knead until you have a dough ball

Roll out dough with rolling pin and cut into your favorite shapes using cookie cutters.

Use grill pan or baking mat inside your air fryer oven to cook dough.

Set the temperature to 360f and cook for 10 minutes.

Allow to cool before serving.

Nutrition:

Calories 271

Fat 15 g

Carbs 33 g

Fiber 1 g

Sugar 26 g

Protein 4 g

50. Mini Cheesecakes

Preparation Time: 15 minutes

Cooking Time: 10 minutes Servings: 2

Ingredients:

¾ cup erythritol

2 eggs

1 teaspoon vanilla extract

½ teaspoon fresh lemon juice

16 oz. Cream cheese, softened

2 tablespoon sour cream

Directions:

In a blender, add the erythritol, eggs, vanilla extract and lemon juice and pulse until smooth.

Add the cream cheese and sour cream and pulse until smooth.

Place the mixture into 2 (4-inch) springform pans evenly.

Press "power button" of air fry oven and turn the dial to select the "air fry" mode. Press the time button and again turn the dial to set the cooking time to 10 minutes.

Now push the temp button and rotate the dial to set the temperature at 350 degrees f. Press "start/pause" button to start. When the unit beeps to show that it is preheated, open the lid.

Arrange the pans in "air fry basket" and insert in the oven. Place the pans onto a wire rack to cool completely. Refrigerate overnight before serving.

Nutrition:

Calories 886

Total fat 86 g

Saturated fat 52.8 g Cholesterol 418 mg

Sodium 740 mg

Total carbs 7.2 g

Fiber 0 g Sugar 1.1 g

Protein 23.1 g

Conclusion

U nlike frying things in a typical pan on gas which fails to make your fries crisp and leaves your samosa uncooked due to uneven heat. The inbuilt kitchen deep fryers do it all; you can have perfectly crisp French fries like the one you get in restaurants. Your samosas will be perfectly cooked inside- out. Well, the list doesn't end here it goes on and on the potato wedges, chicken and much more. You can make many starters and dishes using fryer and relish the taste buds of your loved ones.

The new air fryers come along with a lot of features, so you don't mess up doing things enjoy your cooking experience. The free hot to set the temperature according to your convenience both mechanically and electronically. Oil filters to reuse the oil and use it for a long run. With the ventilation system to reduce and eliminate the frying odor. In a few models you also get the automatic timers and alarm set for convenient cooking, frying I mean. Also, the auto- push and raise feature to immerse or hold back the frying basket to achieve the perfect frying aim. So, why should you wait? I am sure you don't want to mess in your kitchen when grilling, baking of frying your food, right? Get yourself an air fryer. Thank you for purchasing this cookbook I hope you will apply all the acquired knowledge productively.

CPSIA information can be obtained
at www.ICGtesting.com
Printed in the USA
BVHW011441100621
609008BV00015B/714